Bug Babies

Catherine Veitch

Heinemann
LIBRARY
Chicago, Illinois

Edited by Daniel Nunn, Rebecca Rissman,
and Catherine Veitch
Designed by Cynthia Della-Rovere
Picture research by Ruth Blair
Production by Victoria Fitzgerald
Originated by Capstone Global Library

Library of Congress Cataloging-in-Publication Data
Veitch, Catherine.
  Bug babies / Catherine Veitch.
     pages cm.—(Animal babies)
  Includes bibliographical references and index.
  ISBN 978-1-4329-7495-4 (hb)
  ISBN 978-1-4329-8420-5 (pb)
  1. Arthropoda—Infancy—Juvenile literature. 2. Worms—
Infancy—Juvenile literature. I. Title.
  QL434.15.V45 2013
  595.1392—dc23   2012033409

Acknowledgments
Dreamstime: Halil I. Inci, 21; Getty Images: Dorling
Kindersley, 6, Heidi & Hans-Juergen Koch/Minden Pictures,
9, Mark Moffett/Minden Pictures, 14; Nature Picture Library:
Kim Taylor, 10, Martin Dohrn, 8, Meul/ARCO, 16, 18, Paul
Harcourt Davies, 1, 13 Right, 23 Middle, Simon Colmer,
22 Top; Shutterstock: Cathy Keifer, 2, 11 Left, 23 Top, D.
Kucharski K. Kucharska, 5 Bottom Right, Dr Morley Read,
19, FloridaStock, 5 Left, 23 Bottom, Gherasim Rares,
15, irin-k, 5 Top Right, James Laurie, 11 Right, Kletr, 20,
kurt_G, Cover, 17, PHOTO FUN, Back Cover, 7, Sim Kay
Seng, 4, Subbotina Anna, 22 Left, Sue Robinson, 12,
Torsten Dietrich, 13 Left, vaklav, 22 Right

We would like to thank Michael Bright for his invaluable help
in the preparation of this book.

Every effort has been made to contact copyright holders
of material reproduced in this book. Any omissions will
be rectified in subsequent printings if notice is given to
the publisher.

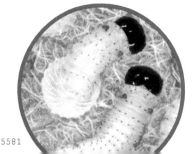

Contents

What Is a Bug?

dragonfly

A bug is a small animal.

spider

insect

worm

Spiders are bugs.

Insects and worms are bugs.

How Are Baby Bugs Born?

eggs

Many bugs lay eggs.

Some bugs lay eggs on soil.

eggs

Some bugs lay eggs
on leaves.

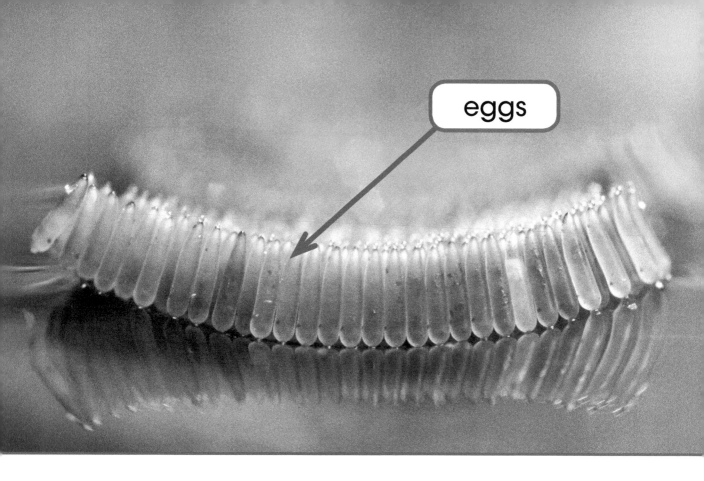

eggs

Some bugs lay eggs on water.

eggs

Some bugs lay eggs on food.

larvae

egg

Larvae can hatch from eggs.

Larvae do not look like their
parents.

nymph

Nymphs can hatch from eggs.

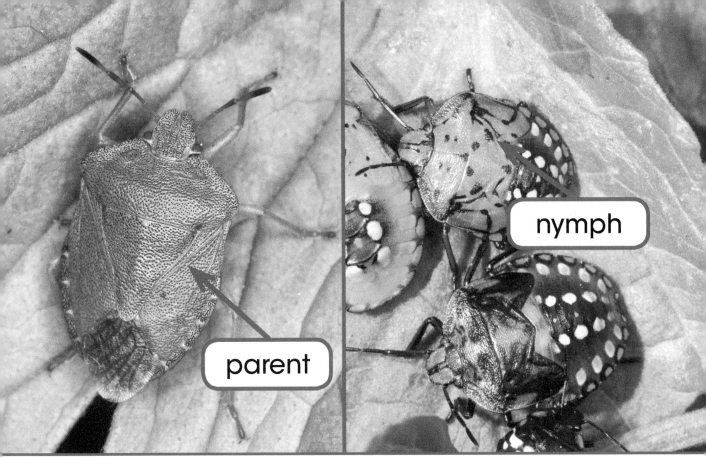

parent

nymph

Nymphs look like their parents.

Caring for Baby Bugs

Some bugs care for
their babies.

larvae

These worker bees bring food to their larvae.

This ant carries its baby to
a safe place.

babies

This spider carries its babies on its back.

Growing Up

Many bug babies care for themselves. Some feed on

smaller bugs.

Some feed on plants.

Some bugs find a new home.

They hide from predators.

Life Cycle of a Bug

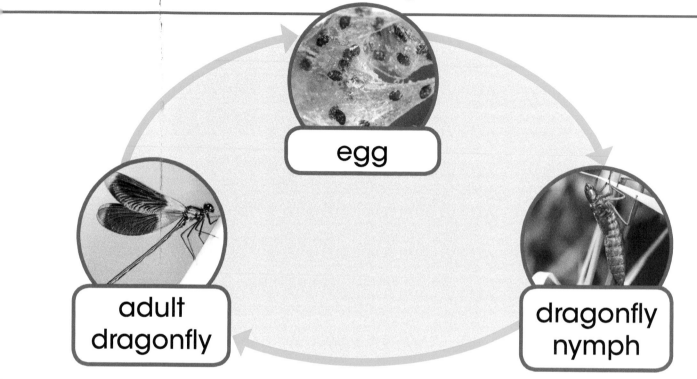

egg

adult dragonfly

dragonfly nymph

A life cycle shows the different stages of an animal's life. This is the life cycle of a dragonfly.

Picture Glossary

 **larva** stage some bugs have when they first hatch. More than one is larvae.

 **nymph** stage some bugs have when they first hatch

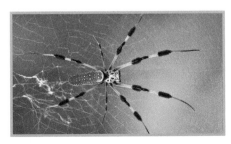 **predator** animal that eats other animals

Index

Notes to Parents and Teachers

Before reading

Show children a collection of photos and videos of bugs. National Geographic and PBS are useful websites. Explain what a bug is and discuss the characteristics of bugs.

After reading

- Mount photos of adult and baby bugs on note cards and play games of concentration where the children have to match a baby bug with its parent. Model the correct pairs first.

- Ask children to label the parts of a bug: for example, wings, head, legs, antennae.

- Look at page 22 and discuss the life cycle stages of a bug. Mount photos of the egg, nymph, and adult stages and ask children to put the photos in order. Encourage children to draw a life cycle of a human to compare. Compare how different bugs care for their babies. Discuss the care human babies need.

- Some children will be curious to learn the names of the bugs. Therefore, to extend children's knowledge, the bugs are as follows: dragonfly: p. 4; spider, ladybug, worm: p. 5; snail eggs: p. 6; butterfly eggs: p. 7; mosquito eggs: p. 8; house fly: p. 9; cabbage white butterfly larvae and eggs: p. 10; monarch butterfly larvae and eggs, monarch butterfly: p. 11; green shield bug nymphs: p. 12; green shield bug parent and nymphs: p. 13; earwig: p. 14; worker bees and larvae: p. 15; yellow mound ant with pupa: p. 16; wolf spider and spiderlings: p. 17; ladybug larvae: p. 18; caterpillar: p. 19; wasp spiderlings: p. 20; caterpillar: p. 21.